MEDITATION
ITS THEORY AND PRACTICE

MEDITATION

ITS THEORY AND PRACTICE

HARI PRASAD SHASTRI

SHANTI SADAN, LONDON

First edition   1936
2nd edition   1938
3rd edition   1942
4th edition   1946
5th edition   1950
Reprinted 1958, 1968, 1971,
1974, 1981, 1987, 1999.

© Shanti Sadan 1999

29 Chepstow Villas London W11 3DR

ISBN 0-85424-006-3

Original setting by Burleigh Press, Bristol.

*Printed and bound by
Print Wright Ltd, Ipswich (01473) 240897*

FOREWORD TO THE FIFTH EDITION

This little book is based on the traditional teachings received by the author from the God-realized Sages of India and China. These teachings are in accord with those found in the holy classics of ancient India, China and Iran, which have been the subject of the author's study for over forty years. They include the science of meditation as taught by Patanjali, Shri Krishna, the Zen Buddhists and the Sufis of Iran.

In this new and completely revised edition, the opportunity has been taken to incorporate additional material from the author's many other writings and lectures on the subject. In this way, the scope of the book has been enlarged and its usefulness enhanced.

The form of the book has also been considerably changed. The first part deals in general terms with the principles of meditation and the spiritual technique of Yoga. In the second part, details are given of some of the practices themselves. Attention has been confined to the simpler preliminary practices, since the descriptions are intended to be of value to those who wish to start meditation for themselves but who may not have had the opportunity, as yet, to obtain the guidance of a teacher. Such guidance is indispensable for the practice of more advanced forms of meditation and Yoga, but an outline of the principles involved is included at the end of this section of the book.

3

CONTENTS

I. THE THEORY OF MEDITATION

II. THE PRACTICE OF MEDITATION

CONTENTS

I
THE THEORY OF MEDITATION

THE PURPOSE OF MEDITATION

> " God-realization is the purpose and goal of life ;
> perfection, everlasting peace and freedom are its
> fruits. When God-realization is once acquired, there
> is no fall from this exalted state of consciousness.
> There is no gain higher than this."
>
> *Shri Mangalnathji.*

WHAT MEDITATION IS

To meditate means, in the preliminary and lower
stages, to apply thought-force *consciously ;* to produce harmony, both within and without ; to obtain
control over the mind and the emotions ; and to
open up the faculty of intuition or *buddhi.*

Our individual minds, conditioned by our bodies,
are but small fractions of the divine or cosmic Mind,
and possess the power of receiving from the cosmic
Mind all that they require for their harmonious
growth. Meditation, therefore, has a spiritual
purpose. The real aim is to acquire a knowledge
of truth and of that spiritual illumination which
recognizes no separateness, which fills the individual
with peace, and inspires him to bring the same light
to others. It leads ultimately to the attainment of
complete freedom from limitations, and the realization of God as one's own Self or *Atman.* This God-
realization is the natural state of the self. The

9

normal state of each individual or soul is perfection in God, and this is the goal of all evolution and progress.

Thus, meditation does not create perfection ; it allows perfection to disclose itself, by removing the obstacles to its realization.   This is a very important point, which must never be forgotten.

MEDITATION AND LIFE

In introducing the reader to the science of meditation—for it is a science—the foundations upon which it stands must first be explained. Meditation cannot be isolated from its place in the body of the spiritual Yoga, and the fundamental principles of Yoga must be grasped if they are to be successfully applied in daily life. It is, therefore, impossible to avoid some excursion into the realm of metaphysics.

Growth and activity are the chief characteristics of life, both on the physical and the spiritual plane. The amoeba's pursuit of nourishment is fundamentally the same urge which causes man to seek truth, although turned to another account and functioning on a far lower level of consciousness. When the life force is directed outwards, it assumes the form of physical activity, but when the same faculty turns inward to its source, then life becomes an emotional, intellectual or spiritual activity. Even the most foolish act has something spiritual about it (its subtle, mental aspect), and a spiritual deed may appear foolish, because we live on these two planes of consciousness at once.

Man is, therefore, an amphibious being. He

derives his inspiration and his values from the contemplative, introspective aspect of his life, and puts them into form in the objective world. The correct attitude towards life is that every man should be subjective for a part of the time. By going deeper and deeper into his own soul, he should discover the real values of life, and on the basis of these values, create something tangible in the objective world.

In meditation, we try to go inward to the Cause, even to that which is sometimes called the " causeless Cause ". Just as a river is purer at its source than it is in the middle or at its mouth, so does the process of meditation become purer and purer as we go back towards the spiritual source. Meditation begins when the mind makes a courageous and determined effort to come into contact with the light of Truth *latent within itself*.

Even the materialists cannot deny to the mind the privilege of receiving inspiration, for the evidence in support of this quoted by William James and others is overwhelming. Virgil was a poet whose inspired verses guided the Emperor Augustus in spreading the spirit of peace far and wide through his dominions. Yet he was a peasant child without education.

The mind requires daily inspiration. The conception behind the word " inspiration " is " something breathed in from above," not from the physical sky but infused transcendentally into a man's mind : something good, beautiful and true, giving guidance to each individual in his walk of life. Inspiration does not mean merely something which confers on us the ability to invent a new kind of motor-car : that is the lowest form of inspiration, if it can be called inspiration at all. True inspiration comes as a thought of power, which can revolutionize society and turn upside down those institutions which are not based on universal good.

In order to know divine Truth, it is essential that we should practise self-restraint and self-abnegation in our daily life. We cannot ignore the ethical side of life and only practise reflection and meditation. If we did so, we should never acquire that inner peace and serenity which gives, not necessarily a life of joy, but joy in life : a joy which enables us to demonstrate the Truth, no matter what may befall us. If this ideal of spiritual peace (*Shanti*) is worth achieving, then we must not neglect our ethical duties.

Concentration should be accompanied by a feeling of resignation or renunciation. Even in physical love, when a lover is really attuned to the object of his love, he not only acquires concentration, but also, if he is fortunate, gives the best in him spiritually to the object of his love. Much depends on the object of love. Romeo loved Juliet : he was concentrated on her and wanted to give up even his life to her. But he remained what he was—he neither became a philosopher or a sage, nor did he do any good to anyone. Perhaps after his death he acquired some proximity to the object of his love, but no deification of the soul, not even a flash of spiritual illumination.

Another point to be remembered is that nothing should be desired in the concrete realm. When you have decided to give up all in favour of God, it is an anomaly if you yearn for anything worldly. Meditation will not be successful if there is desire or aversion, love or hate for any object of the world present in your heart. Meditation is a continuous practice, and the only result that you should expect from it is a love of goodness and truth, and indifference to the passing objects of the world.

The preliminary stages on the path to proficiency in meditation are :

First. REPENTANCE : that is, the realization of one's shortcomings and the earnest effort to rise above them.

Second. ABSTINENCE from what one thinks wrong and from what degrades one in one's own eyes.

Third. RENUNCIATION : that is, giving up the sense of possession, whether of material things or of affections.

Fourth. AUSTERITY : that is, making one's material needs as simple as possible. Austerity does not imply want ; no one should want ; want harasses the soul.

Fifth. TRUST IN GOD : that is, patience in the face of the ills of life. Take everything that comes as from God, and it will become your friend. Be like the mystic *Rabi'a*, whose prayers healed many but who never tried to heal herself, saying : " All comes from Him Who is my Friend " that is, " All comes from God".

BEAUTY AND TRUTH

Everyone loves. The question is, what do we love ? Some love their children, some love a friend, some are philanthropists and love all men, some love an ideal, and some love abstract ideas. In fact, we really only love one thing, and that is Beauty. Some love the beauty of nature, some love beautiful pictures, others beautiful poetry or music. One of the highest aspects of beauty, and one that appeals to all, is beauty of character.

Real beauty must have a certain vagueness : you will remember that Aphrodite was created out of the foam of the sea. When we know all about a person and there is nothing left to discover, interest becomes exhausted, and we cease to love.

God is incomprehensible in the sense that, although we can come to know Him, we can never fathom the depths and heights, or understand all that there is to know of God, for He transcends all. The Sufi word for God is " Beauty," not the beautiful, but Beauty Absolute.

It is the greatest mistake to give our love to the beautiful, instead of to Beauty. You often hear parents say that they wish their baby could always remain two or three years old. They love the beauty of babyhood but Beauty eludes them. The man who is trying to love the beautiful is a beggar begging at his own door, for it is that God within him Who appears as the waves, the grass, the great tropical rivers reflecting the sky, the flowers, the mountains and every beautiful object.

What then, is ugliness ? Who can say ? Where you see ugliness, I may see beauty, and vice versa. As with heat and cold, it is a matter of degree, and we are not the final judges of what is ugly. To see the beauty of pictures or music requires a certain training, but the whole world is an overflowing of the beauty of God, Who is Beauty Absolute ; and all can see something of this Beauty, and when they see it, they love. We all have the capacity to love, but the heart of man is never satisfied until it goes beyond beautiful conceptions and turns to God.

There are many veils which hide Beauty. Indeed it is said that seventy thousand veils hide Truth, and Truth is another name for Beauty. You may say that it is too difficult to penetrate so deeply, but every soul is on a pilgrimage to discover Beauty Absolute, and one must cultivate a love for difficult things.

According to the Yogic teaching, there are three conceptions which rend these veils, and each tears asunder one third of them.

The first conception is : " There is One God ". This was the cry raised by holy Abraham over five thousand years ago, and re-echoed by Mohammed and others. " There is no God but Allah." He alone is the one God, the only Lord of all the Universes. There is no other Lord. Akhnaton, the Pharoah of Egypt in the fourteenth century B.C., also declared this truth. They thought of God as One, because they wished to establish the truth of Unity, which those who worshipped many gods failed to realize.

What is the meaning of this doctrine ? It means that all life is one, and that, because it is one, we are all vitally affected by everything which takes place in it. To know this, rends asunder one third of the veils.

The man who has come to know that all is God,

knows something about God, and he then begins to say : " There is no God but Thou ! Thou alone art ! Thou art all ! " This is the second stage, and this consciousness rends asunder another third of the veils. We come to this knowledge after we have realized the first third of the mystery—that God is One, and that One, All. When we have penetrated the second third of the veils and have discovered that God is " Thou ", a new intoxication comes to us. With the use of the word " Thou", a fresh relationship opens to us, and a profound happiness flows over us, accompanied by a great love for all.

The writer remembers an occasion when a holy man was meditating on God. He was surrounded by many people. Suddenly, a snake appeared and some of the crowd tried to kill it. But the man who had been meditating on God as " Thou alone art " told them not to do so and, taking up the snake, twined it round his neck to give it the protection of his love. That man had known God as " Thou ".

The last third of the veils is rent when we know God as " I ". It was thus that Jesus knew God. " I and my Father are One ", " He who hath seen Me hath seen the Father." These were His words, and so deep was this knowledge in Him, that often He did not need to speak of God, but spoke only of " I ". He said " Come unto Me, all ye who labour and are heavy laden, and I will give you rest ". There are many similar sayings of His recorded in the Gospels. Only when we know God as " I " is love complete.

There was an Indian saint who daily used to offer flowers to God, but the time came when he put flowers on his own head, offering them to himself, as he said over and over again : " *Shivoham Shivoham* "—" I am God ! I am God ! "

How are we to begin to tear away these veils ? First of all, we must love. Everyone must love something. Love something — anything — even though it be only a worldly ideal to start with, but you must love. If you love, then this worldly love may lead to something higher.

REASON, INTUITION, VISION

There are three faculties bestowed by God on man, by which he can acquire a knowledge of Truth. They are : Reason, Intuition, and spiritual Vision. Each represents a different way of approach, but in reality they are three aspects of the same thing, three facets of the prism which is man.

By means of the discursive reason or intellect, man can enquire into truth, and discover the nature of a thing in terms of its relation to other objects. Reason functions in the world of duality and its purpose is to synthesise differences. The spiritual faculty of intuition, however, can transcend reason. All discoveries are made in the end, not through the reason, but by that faculty of the soul called intuition (*buddhi*). Reason very often prepares the way, but the great leap in the dark is always taken by intuition, through meditation. Columbus knew of a land beyond the seas not through reason, but through intuition ; he had long meditated on an idea to which reason had originally led him.

Meditation brings into action the faculty of intuition (*buddhi*) and it is this mystical sense which gives us the capacity to approach the absolute Truth. Hume maintains that Truth is inaccessible and unapproachable but this is not so. The Sufis and the Indian and Jewish mystics all declare that Truth is knowable, and teach this way of approach. The faculty which can apprehend truth is not special to a privileged few ; it is latent in all, in the sinner and in the saint.

By cultivating intuition, we can meditate on God, but to do so, we must leave the discursive reason on one side for the time being. In order to *know* God, even intuition is not enough ; there is yet another faculty to be aroused—that of vision. Unless we *see* God, we shall not know Him, and the spirit of man *can* see God. The word " see " is perhaps not the right one, but it appears to be the best that we can use. We *see ;* we *know ;* we *realize ;* this is absolute knowledge, direct experience, whereby God becomes real to us, and in us.

The spirit of man is God in a conditioned form. It is only this element in man, his real Self (*Atman*), which can know God.

When this knowledge of God, or Self-realization, comes, then there follows that spiritual peace which is called *Shanti* in Sanskrit and *Salem* by the Jews. Those who have acquired the realization of this spiritual peace can bear witness to the Truth, calm and undaunted, even under a shower of bullets. If their dearest friend betrays them, they are like a great mountain, immovable in the midst of storm, with its highest peak lit by the dazzling sunlight.

We are here in the world to realize this perfect peace and freedom, and when it is attained, life becomes worthwhile. Then the bird's song finds an echo in our hearts, and all the loveliness of nature is but a reflection of that which is within our souls. Meditation is one of the ways by which this peace and joy is to be obtained.

There is a difference between knowledge and meditation. Knowledge is spontaneous. Whether you desire to see the full moon riding in the heavens, or whether you do not desire to see it, you will certainly do so ; in either case, you have the spontaneous knowledge that the moon is there. There are those who do not like to hear thunder, but they are sometimes compelled to experience it, whether they will or no.

It is written : " Without *knowledge* there is no salvation ", not, " Without *meditation* there is no salvation ". Meditation *per se* is valueless. It is merely the method whereby the knowledge of God-realization is attained, and herein lies its real value. Meditation itself is a technique for purifying the psychological instruments of knowledge, and for awakening their faculty of spiritual intuition.

THE PRINCIPLES OF MEDITATION

Meditation is based on certain fundamental laws, which must be recognized before any attempt is made to practise it.

PHYSICAL, MENTAL AND SPIRITUAL FORCE

Thought is a creative force. Actions are materialized thoughts, and thought-force, although inferior to spiritual force, is much more potent than physical force. It is also less conditioned by time and space than is physical force, but in fact neither physical nor mental force can prevail over spiritual force.

A good illustration of this fact can be seen in Chinese history. The Mongols were a great danger and terror to China. The Great Wall was built, fourteen hundred miles long, to keep them out of the country, but it proved useless. It was the spiritual force of China which finally transformed the Mongols from a fierce and violent race into a peace-loving people. On the borders of Mongolia the Emperor K'ang Hsi established Buddhist monasteries with libraries and really learned and saintly monks, centres of peace and devotion. He entertained the Mongol princes and gave them the benefit of the Buddhist teachings. The result was that, within fifty years, the Mongols threw down their arms and never again invaded China. In this way, the Emperor K'ang Hsi educated the Mongols. Force on the physical plane, represented by the Great Wall, could not accomplish the desired result, whereas spiritual education achieved it. Spiritual power will manifest naturally of itself if the heart is pure, and meditation is the means whereby the heart is purified.

CHARACTERISTICS AND NATURE OF THE MIND

The character or " personality " of an individual is usually the result of his or her thoughts, and character can be modified by consciously directed thought. This is an important point. Like everything else in nature, the mind is in a constant state of vibration, and these vibrations are called " thoughts " or " *vrittis*". These *vrittis* passing through the senses, act upon matter, their chief function being to perceive, to appreciate, to evaluate, modify and analyse.

Mind is a great creative force, and its creativeness comes into operation in a condition of perfect silence. Accumulation of energy leads to creation. When we sit in meditation, we stop our senses from functioning, and an accumulation of mental energy is stored up in the psychic region. Invisible forces come into play, inspiration wells up and the imagination becomes refined in its function. The mind when stilled becomes creative, but in order to create spiritual forms of everlasting beauty, like Dante's epic, Kalidas's Shakuntala, or the spiritual peace (*Shanti*) of Yoga, it must also be illumined. The mind imbibes the quality of its experience: it is, in a sense, like a wax tablet on which past impressions are recorded. It thus receives impressions, not only through the senses but also from the store of past thoughts and feelings, which emerge under the incentive of kindred association. This store is the seat of memory and imagination, and it is continually being replenished. Our present character is thus very much influenced by our past thoughts, and it is essential to realize that what we interest ourselves in and feel strongly about at the present time, sinks into the substance of the mind and will return to us intensified in the future. We must, therefore, be discriminating in the matter of our thoughts.

The ideas spontaneously offered by the mind are the outcome of such past impressions (*sanskaras*). These ideas, which manifest themselves in the form of impulses, likes and dislikes, are blind, and to accept and execute them without critical examination is not in accordance with man's nature as a rational being. Mental suggestions once uncritically accepted turn in the course of time into dictation by the mind.

The mind is like a bird in a field, always pecking at and picking up something ; what is important is that it should select wisely. All that the senses report is woven into something which tends either to destroy or to build up the mind, for the mind assimilates that upon which it dwells. If it broods on crime, then it will become filled with a store of that quality of thought.

Yoga does not believe in killing any part of our psychological instrument : its aim is to train, transform and use it in the right way. It is clear that we cannot live the best life unless our mind is tranquillised, for only then does it receive the divine light from its original source within the personality. Hatred and fanaticism introduce qualities which coarsen the mind, impairing mental health ; but selfless thoughts are pure, for they seek the well-being of all and unite the puny individual mind with the cosmic Mind, the mind of God, which rules alike the stars in their courses, the electrons in their orbits, and governs the emergence of the infinitely varied forms of life.

Modern psychologists like Jung agree that minds are, in reality, not individual ; that the cosmic Mind is a single mind which has become locally encased in individuality. Our individual minds, conditioned by our bodies, are therefore but small fractions of the cosmic Mind, with which they must put themselves into conscious relationship if they are to develop harmoniously.

EMPTYING THE MIND

Meditation means, amongst other things, the tranquillisation and purification of the mind. The ground must be prepared for this by the expulsion from the mind of all that is mean and degrading, all that does not promote the well-being of society and the individual. All thoughts of duality and separation, and also all desires which impede spiritual progress must be carefully eliminated, and harboured no more.

A good illustration of the necessity for emptying the mind of its contents is given in a *Zen* story. There was in Japan a *Zen* monk who was an adept in meditation. Among the men from all walks of life who were attracted by his reputation as a teacher, was a well-known Professor of the Imperial University of Tokyo. The Professor went to see the monk, who offered him the customary green tea. Placing a cup before the distinguished visitor, he poured tea into it until it became full. He continued to pour, and the cup overflowed. Seeing the tea spilling over the table and on to the floor-mats, the startled Professor asked for an explanation. The *Zen* monk said : " I can fill what is empty, but not that which is already full. You have come to me with your mind full of ideas of *meum* and *tuum*, ambitions and desires. If you seek my instruction, empty your mind, forget all you have learnt, and rid yourself of all harmful and useless matter; then return and I will teach you."

Alas ! We usually fill our minds with desires, many of which are pernicious and bring nothing but evil, and with passions which blind us to the great spiritual beauty exhibited by such men as Jesus, Shankaracharya, Aristotle and Goethe. Sense pleasures are the most dangerous factor in our lives. Materialism is not such a formidable enemy to us as is sensualism, which has for its main objective the extraction of pleasure from external objects. This prevents us from assessing values correctly, and causes us to see darkness where there is light, and vice versa.

RESTRAINT OF THE SENSES

To dwell with delight on sense-objects gives rise to an attachment to them, and this attachment, when thwarted, breeds anger, as the Gita teaches. It leads to desire for personal acquisition and selfish enjoyment. Let us take an example. A child sees a doll in a shop window and says to herself : " How beautiful it is ; what lovely eyes it has ; how lovely it would be to hold it, and to show it to Paul and Dinah. Oh ! it *is* lovely ! " Each time the child dwells on the doll with delight, she is driving its image deeper and deeper into her mind. It is acquiring a stronger hold on her and will soon occupy a prominent place in her life ; it is beginning to exclude from her heart other objects of beauty, thus localizing and weakening her consciousness. She asks her mother to buy the doll, but is told that she cannot afford it. Finding that she will not get the doll, the child becomes sad and she is angry with her mother. Being so pre-occupied with the toy, she forgets the respect due to her parents, the importance of truth and so forth. This is called, in the Gita, " loss of memory ", meaning not a weak memory but forgetfulness of the law of righteousness (*dharma*).

The primary cause of all this misery was the harbouring of pleasant thoughts about the doll, an object of pleasure. Therefore, the need for detachment is stressed in Yoga training. In the Gita, it says : " In sense objects see suffering ". This does not mean that you should adopt pessimism as your rule of life, but that you should realize that each object which attracts you and overpowers your sense of discrimination does immense damage to your nature. The deeper the infatuation, the greater the harm wrought. It is a mistake to become mad over anything in the world, or to allow any object to possess you. Thus is suffering produced ; yet there is no need for anyone in this world to suffer, because sufferings are self-invited. The mind was never meant to be the seat of worldly passions—desire, lust, anger, and (worst of all) hatred. To give way to anger or to express hatred is to stab, as with a dagger, the fine silken texture of the mind's surface, the surface which should reflect the light of the divine Mind.

Suffering is an indication of want of inner balance. The path to peace lies through harmony. Our emotions should harmonize with our reason, and our reason with the dictates of the divine Mind. When complete harmony prevails in the personality, forms evolve harmoniously, whereas want of harmony expresses itself in the physical world as disease, and in the mental world as ignorance, with its offshoots, fear, anxiety and so forth.

Picture a glacier stretching for miles on the high hills, from which issue thousands of small streams, flowing far and wide. The glacier is the universal Mind (or the divine Mind, as I call it). There is but one Mind, and our individual minds are like the streamlets which issue from It. If the flow of pure water is dammed up, the streams become stagnant. Similarly, sense-pleasures and love of power and comfort cut us off from the supreme Source. It is essential that there should be an unimpeded flow from the divine glacier within us into our consciousness. The process of removing obstructions is called prayer and meditation : it is their function to preserve a clear channel for the Divine to flow into the individual. Therefore, the individuality in which our mind is imprisoned must be rendered transparent. The thing which prevents this—the great barrier which makes individuality so miserably narrow and opaque—is the love of pleasure and power. As has been said, the texture of the mind is coarsened and rendered opaque by narrowness, prejudice and all selfishness and accentuation of egoity. The mind must be made light throughout all its layers, that is, throughout the instinctive, emotional, intellectual, intuitional and spiritual planes. This is done by admitting into it only the purest desires and the purest thoughts, and by practising meditation and contemplation so that the quietened mind may offer no impediment to the divine flow. When the mind is ruled in this way, it becomes a boon to ourselves and others.

II.
THE PRACTICE OF MEDITATION

ELEMENTARY MEDITATION

PRELIMINARY PRACTICES.

In order to practise meditation or Yoga, you are not asked to sit specializing in breathing exercises, for these are in many cases not only unhelpful but actually harmful; they require a special diet, a special mode of life, otherwise they may tell upon the physical system. Do not resort to them, but turn through prayer, devotion and meditation to the omnipotent Lord within you, Who is willing to take twenty steps towards you for every step you take towards Him.

Yoga is not designed to kill any part of the psychological instrument, but its aim is to train, transform and use that instrument in the right way. Illness, failure, misfortune and other negative conditions resulting from past actions (*Karma*) are subject to modification through concentrated and purified thought, but although it is good to have health, prosperity and other advantages in life, they mean very little if they are not accompanied by peace of mind and the desire to be of service to our fellow-men. A fit physical vehicle is indeed an asset, and it has been found that success in meditation is assisted by giving up, if not all meat, at least beef, the eating of which coarsens the texture of the mind, through which the influx of divine life will be received.

The body, however, cannot be kept in a fit condition by exercise and diet alone. It is the mind which serves and maintains the body, and, as has already been pointed out, in order to be healthy it must be restrained, purified and tranquillised. *Restraint* of the mind is essential to preserve it from entering channels likely to place it in bondage. *Purity* is essential for its proper growth. *Tranquillity* is essential in order that the divine Light may be reflected, and radiated by the mind.

If the meditations do not bring peace, if they fail to inspire us with benevolence, compassion, devotion and a love of Truth, they are not spiritual. By performing the practices daily, you should find peace. Assuredly, you *will* find peace. If you do not find it, then look for the fault in your own self. There is a great lesson to be learnt from the sage Confucius who taught : " If an archer misses the target he finds no fault with the target, nor with the bow, nor with the arrow, but with himself alone." So, if you act in this manner, locating the cause of failure in your own self, one day the imperfections will vanish and the divine forces will quicken within you. In this way, anyone and everyone can become inspired, a God-man, steeped in peace, and devoted to the good of all.

It has already been pointed out that to meditate means (in the preliminary and lower stages) to apply thought force *consciously*, in order to obtain control over the mind and emotions ; to produce harmony within, and to open up the faculty of intuition (*buddhi*).

In this connection it should be noted that emotional force is stronger than thought force, and stronger than either is the power of the will. In meditation, we begin with thought; then we pass into the realm of the emotions, and finally into the region of the will.

In order to meditate, the first essential is to forget the objective world entirely. It is not enough to concentrate—concentration is merely a preliminary state. The real purpose of contemplation is that the mind shall be withdrawn from outer objects, and also from the inner concepts (the stream of ideas and feelings), and then focused on one point. The practice has a double purpose: to create a vacuum in the mind, and to fill that vacuum with what is desirable.

The mind interferes with meditation by bringing before us pictures and various memories. Very often as one sits in meditation such distractions will arise, and perhaps some advertisement which one has seen in an Underground, or some children one has played with in a garden, or some other object, will intrude into the solitude of the mind. But the will is stronger than either thought or mind, and can banish these pictures. Fill the mind so completely with the idea of the meditation, that no room is left in it for anything else. Continue negating the distractions and gently lead the mind back to the meditation.

For the meditation, take a certain text—the student of Yoga usually takes one recommended by his *Guru* (or spiritual Teacher)—and while meditating on it, discipline and tranquillise the mind by the will, in order that the text may gradually sink into the consciousness. It is not enough to meditate for twenty or thirty minutes each morning, and then to allow the mind to run riot for the rest of the day, for this is only to fashion Penelope's web, which she wove in the day and unravelled every evening so that no progress was made.

Make it a point to be calm throughout the day. Whatever happens, treat everyone with sympathy and kindness, and be assured that there are no enemies in the world, unless they are self-created ; there are no strangers either. The divine life is one and the same, manifesting in everyone, saints and sinners alike. You can establish contact with this divine life when your power of meditation has reached a certain pitch : then you will find a change in your whole life. If you have occasion to think anyone is your enemy, you must cover him with the choicest blessings. Our friendships need as much repair as our shoes. We have to be universal in the charity of our thought, for from heaven to earth there is only one force, one substratum that creates the magic of all phenomena—and it is one's own Self. This is the essence of the philosophy of Plato, Schiller, Fichte and Hegel. What if anyone abuses you ? The Chinese sage *Lao Tzu* has said : " I am kind to those who are kind to me—and still good to those who are not." Unless you live your daily life according to this principle, your meditation and general spiritual life will not be in harmony with the creative spiritual force.

Carry a copy of the *Bhagavad-Gita* : study it and mould your life on its threefold ideal :—(1) *Undisturbability* : this is a characteristic of the British people, and was the basis of their real greatness in the last war. (2) *True identification* : however active you may be, never forget that you are not the body, or the mind, but something far greater—for you are the eternal and ever-blissful Spirit. All your actions should be of such a nature that they develop this consciousness in you. Such a way of life is a perpetual prayer ; mere transitory prayer is ineffectual. (3) *Truth* : Choose the holy Name which, through its associations, most appeals to you ; either Jesus, if you love it, or Rama or OM or simply Truth—for Truth is God. Just as Romeo was mentally infatuated by the form of Juliet, which in an unguarded moment had taken possession of his mind—a mind which should have been possessed by Truth—so let a holy Name possess your heart all the time.

Protect your mind from outer influences more carefully than you would protect a rare diamond. Be discriminative in your reading and in your eating. The time will come when you will become aware that the spirit of God, or Truth, is quickening within you. Then darkness will be dissipated as the fog melts in a valley before the rising sun; rich then will be your life, and you will bless yourself and humanity.

If the mind is brought by meditation into closer and closer proximity with its spiritual source or cause, certain changes take place in it, but as has been pointed out, these changes will not endure and are likely to lapse if we do not take care of our

35

thoughts and mental outlook during the rest of the day. It must be with us as it is with the true athlete: he practises at certain times during the day, but maintains a kind of rhythm and lightness of limb the whole time. So, one who meditates must apply the harmony and peace that he experiences at the time of meditation throughout the hours of activity.

We must think of God as often as possible, and render thanks to Him. However the text of the meditation may be worded, we must never divorce it from God, Who is Truth. God is our aim; He is all in all, and the supreme goal and object of our meditations.

You will perhaps question whether life can be lived thus, in perpetual recollection of the Highest? Yes! The importance lies, not in action, but in the understanding and interpretation of action. The interpretation of life must be spiritual. There is a story of a certain Japanese Empress, who went into her garden one summer morning and found it a carpet of the most lovely flowers. She exclaimed: " O beautiful flowers! You have come from the bosom of the Buddha, you reflect the beauty of the Buddha, and I dedicate you to the Buddha." If she had had any sense of possession, she could not have done this, and the spiritual significance of the experience would have been lost.

How to Meditate.

Sit quietly, in the morning if possible, in a comfortable, firm position, either on a chair or preferably on a cushion placed on the floor. The spine, neck and head should be kept erect in a straight line with the chin held in. To attempt to meditate sitting up in bed is not at all propitious as the associations of bed are far too inert and negative, and in meditation one should be alert, though mentally peaceful.

The best times for meditation are the early morning and before retiring at night, but whatever hour and place is decided upon should be maintained if humanly possible, because a rhythm is thus established and a spiritual habit formed which increases the power and effectiveness of the meditation. Thus, sitting in relaxation, concentrate your thoughts on the spot between the two eyebrows, which is a most important centre of consciousness. The body is like a ship steered through the sea of life by the mind, who is the captain of the ship, and who directs it from this spot between the brows, which may be likened to the bridge. Universal consciousness itself is located in this centre, though this fact must not be confused with the position of the glands of the physical body, which function on a lower plane of consciousness.

Concentrate and locate the mind on this spot. Then place there the name of Jesus Christ or of Buddha, according to your faith. If your religious beliefs are not identified with either of these great figures, or even if you believe in no one at all, it does not matter ; their place can be taken by the word of Power—OM—the symbol of all that is highest and most beautiful. In perfect relaxation, centre your mind on the Name for five to seven minutes. For a few days, you may feel bored and find no satisfaction in the practice, but you will have to be patient and persevering in your endeavour. If you do this practice for forty days, without expecting any tangible results, you will find a new light quickening in your mind, and your thoughts will take a new direction. Concentrate on Truth—all-pervading and eternal—and make it the dearest object in your life.

Once a day, at an appointed time, make a thorough and dispassionate self-examination, and note carefully your chief weaknesses of character. Be a severe judge of yourself, without any emotional despondency, and set aside all your prejudices. Do not attribute anything to chance or fate ; realise that you make of yourself what you will.

Every day take one of your weaknesses and resolve to overcome it. Do not repent, do not be sorry about it, but just resolve to master it. Exercise your will-power to calm your mind, and say several times to yourself :

" I, the master of my own thoughts and emotions, hereby resolve to overcome . . . . and I command my mind to banish it. I know that I can do so, and I will. Nothing can prevent me from mastering it. May God, who is my higher Self, help me."

Now decide which virtue is the exact opposite of the weakness you wish to eradicate, and meditate on that. This involves excluding all other thoughts from the mind. Try to do this and keep this virtue steadily before you.

Devote, if possible, at least half an hour a day to

this exercise ; do it at the same time every day, and do it with interest. Do not be disappointed if you are not successful at first.

Before going to bed at night, examine yourself to see how far success has attended your efforts. Merge your mind in the qualities of courage, self-reliance and strength.

Suggestion and auto-suggestion have a great effect on the mind. By auto-suggestion, your will-power is increased : a strong and resolute will is developed by visualizing success. Auto-suggestion is the mother of a strong will ; any habit can be formed or broken by training the will through auto-suggestion. After a fortnight, most of your bad habits can be broken.

Avoid all hurry and needless anxiety during the day, and remain in a peaceful state of mind. Think of strength and feel that you are becoming stronger and stronger. Be kind and considerate to all, but do not preach. If you start preaching in the initial stages of meditation, you will lose the power of concentration, so do not try to reform others until you have reformed yourself to a considerable degree. The best way to help mankind is to let the good flow from you unconsciously.

It is also desirable to take an interest in poetry, music and art, but care should be taken to see that what you read is really good, and has an uplifting and spiritual quality. Beauty raises the soul to God, Who is the Fountain-head of all beauty and bliss. Enjoy this beauty as a master, and not as a slave ; if you do so, you will feel spiritual exaltation and be the means of bringing peace to those who come into touch with you. If you suddenly meet with an unpleasant experience, do not be upset and never lose faith in your strength.

To be master of yourself, you must love truth above all. All diplomacy must give way to it. No progress in meditation is of any value if it does not lead to the love of truth. Avoid all associations where truth is sacrificed.

SUBJECTS FOR MEDITATION

A series of four meditations is now given, each set complete in itself. The first should be done daily for at least a fortnight, and when some facility has been acquired in it, and it can be done in relaxation, the second can be taken up, and so on throughout the series.

I

Posture

Sit on a carpet or blanket on a level piece of ground; not on a bed. Sit still, with the back, head and neck in a straight line. When you sit in this position, the vital cosmic force which is vibrating through every atom of creation, affects your nerves and mental system, without let or hindrance. To sit in this posture, in relaxation, tranquillizes the mind.

Breathing

Focus the mind on the navel. Take a deep breath in relaxation, and, as you breathe in, imagine that you are drawing the breath up from the navel, so that you end the breath by thinking of the space between the eyebrows. Take twenty-one breaths in this way. Man is a replica of the Universe : as there are solar systems and galactic and other systems in the Universe, so are they represented in man. Not only that, but there is a direct correspondence between man and all the centres of the Universe. As God is said to dwell in Heaven, although He is all-pervasive, so does He dwell in the heart of man, in His personal form, and in the centre of the brain, in His impersonal form. When you have taken the twenty-one breaths in relaxation and have opened up your physiological and mental structures to the whole Universe, with which they are connected, you will feel a kind of peace, a kind of delight, which is not created by contact of the senses with any object.

Meditation

Visualize any sunrise you may have seen, imagine the sun is rising higher and higher over the mountains, over the trees, over the plains. Concentrate on this picture for at least five minutes. If this can be done for a longer period, greater benefit will be derived. There is a significant correspondence between the physical source of light and the inner source of light. There are references to this fact in all religious classics.

Draw the breath again slowly from navel to eyebrows twenty-one times, and with each breath say silently : " I am bliss ; I am bliss."

Forgive anyone against whom you may have a grievance, and during the day keep in relaxation while you do whatever you have to do.

II

Sit in the correct meditation posture and in relaxation, and take twenty-one breaths as before.

Put the following thought before the mind : " I am (my real Spirit is) an eternally blazing fire. All thoughts and desires are sparks radiating from me. OM." The technique for putting the thought into the mind is to put the meditation before you, and think you are taking the statement in on a long breath. Then stop and breathe out. Breathe in again, thinking you are taking the statement and its meaning into your mind. After a few breaths, the meditation rests in the mind. If during the meditation the mind thinks of something else, gently bring it back and do not be annoyed. The mind is like a restless child, so it is no use being angry with it ; and with practice, the meditation becomes continuous. Hold the thought for more than five minutes.

End by giving your blessing to those who you think hate you or are against you.

III

Sit in relaxation, in the meditation posture. Think of the navel and place, in your imagination, the word OM there. For a few minutes just think of OM on the navel, then breathe slowly up and down rhythmically for fully five minutes, concentrating the attention the whole time on the OM on the navel.

Draw an imaginary line of light from the top of the forehead, down between the eyebrows, down the nose, lips, throat, heart-region to the navel. Imagine this line to be a line of light, and concentrate on it for ten minutes. In the beginning, you can draw your finger down the line, if it helps you to visualize it. Then sit and just think of this line of light. This is a very important practice, and is called the Madhyam practice. The results are not physiological, but relate to the vital energy, *prana*. If you do this practice every day, your mind will keep itself away from evils. To conquer passions, to overcome anger, pleasure-sense and pride, do this practice, and you will not be subject to the evil of anyone. The practice is both protective and defensive. A great *Acharya* (spiritual teacher) says : " In the middle of the stream no poisonous plants grow, only on the banks." In the same way, when the flow of consciousness is kept in the middle on this line, no evil will grow in the soul.

At first, this practice should only be done at the time of meditation, but when some facility is gained in it, it can be done all the time, wherever you go and whatever you are doing.

IV

Sit in the meditative posture. Place OM on the navel, and breathe in and out slowly, twenty-one times, bringing the breath up to the head as before.

After taking the twenty-one breaths in complete relaxation, the obstructions and agitations which hinder meditation will disappear. When you are relaxed, then creation takes place in the heart.

Now sit and think. Give free scope to your mind to think, but whatever idea the mind brings before you, say : " It is an illusion. I do not want it." As you sit quiet, the seeds of thought, sown by you, and which have passed into the unconscious, begin to appear in your mind, according to the law of association. When they appear, reject them by this method. When the first thought comes before you, say : " It is illusory." When the next thought comes, perhaps a remembrance of something you have seen, say : " It is illusory." When the next thought comes, perhaps the desire to make a name, to be famous, say : " This is all illusory, this too is all illusion." After about ten minutes you will begin to think consciously. If this practice is done for twenty-one days, you will notice a great change, and your thinking will become constructive.

The following meditation is to be done as the final practice :

" OM. God pervades the inner and outer life. God is truth, beauty, bliss and peace. OM."

Take this meditation into the mind as before, and sitting in relaxation, let the mind be filled with it.

FURTHER PRACTICES

Here are a few other subjects for meditation : with explanations and instructions how to carry them out.

MEDITATION: ITS THEORY AND PRACTICE

I

" OM. O my mind find rest in the most blessed
peace which is always within thee, and follow not after
that which is transient."

This kind of meditation may be called educational,
for it educates the mind spiritually, and if done
properly the mind will receive a measure of the
true spiritual peace. In this way, tranquillity and
righteousness become a part of the empirical nature.

When the meditation has been held in the mind
for some time, it passes into the emotions, and *it is
here that the real seeds of meditation are sown.* The sage
Shri Vyasa has said :

" In the beginning, meditation simply means the
concentration of the mind on a pure spiritual idea ;
but when it is concentrated enough, then the idea
passes into the emotions."

Sometimes there is a difficulty : the mind cannot
concentrate long enough on the idea. On this point,
Shri Vyasa has stated :

" As long as the mind dwells on something akin to
the idea of the meditation, the meditation is complete
(unbroken)."

For example : I take a vase of flowers on which
to meditate. I may think of the seeds and the marvel
of the plants growing from them, the bursting buds
of spring, the loveliness of the newly-opened flowers
or even of the hands that arranged them—all this
is part of the meditation. Though the mind may
stray, if one returns to the initial subject very soon,
the meditation is not spoilt.

When the meditation passes into the realm of the emotions (*Chitta*), the discursive and analytical functions of the mind will be suspended. The mind criticises and chooses, analyses and reasons, but when the meditation goes into *Chitta*, all this ceases and there is no longer any consciousness of time and place.

II

(a) Breathe in, filling the mind with the conception of love and compassion. Do this nineteen times, disregarding the outgoing breaths.

(b) Breathe out, filling your mind with the conception of beauty, goodness and perfection. Do this nineteen times, disregarding the indrawn breaths.

(c) Imagine that you are sending out a blue light from the crown of your head. Stand erect facing the East while doing this meditation.

It is said that if this meditation is correctly practised for forty days, the one who has done so can visit the sick and the suffering and bring peace and relief to them by his mere presence.

III

The mind is now to be concentrated on an aspect of God. There are two aspects of God: one is the concrete and the other the abstract aspect. You can meditate on either, but usually the first-named is a preliminary to the second. The abstract aspect of God is His nature as supreme Beauty, Consciousness and Truth.

In the concrete meditation, learn to focus your

mind on the child Krishna, or Jesus. Visualize the object of meditation, and think of it with all love, imagining yourself to be near it. Then think of what you are and what you have, and offer it all to the object of your love. This is a very good practice, and if done with devotion, concentration and continuity, will lead to illumination in a short time.

IV

Make a picture of one of the great *Avatars* (Incarnations) such as Krishna, Buddha, Jesus Christ, and dwell on it. Sometimes take one, sometimes another, for the mind likes variety. Think of these great Ones; read about them; pour out your love on them and try to imitate them. It is good to hear and read about the *Avatars* and to identify ourselves with them, for by so doing, our whole being becomes filled with their spirit, and we transmute our emotions into Light. But it is mere sentimentalism to talk about Christ or Buddha if we do not try to manifest their love, their tolerance and their mercy.

It is desirable and good to meditate thus on Krishna, Christ or Buddha, but to meditate on the Infinite *Brahman* (God) in all His fullness and perfection, ever remembering that the Avatars were rays of Him Who is the Whole, is the best practice of all.

V

Imagine yourself sitting on the grass on a mountain side, clothed in a white robe and surrounded by others, also in white. Imagine that you are listening to Christ preaching the Sermon on the

47

Mount. Listen to His words, and realize that He is addressing them to you.

VI

If you desire to meditate on Beauty, make a picture of what, to you, is the most beautiful object —the sky, mountains, peacocks—anything the beauty of which moves you deeply. Dwell on this picture for a while, then realize that it is God whom you love in the object, that God is hidden beneath and by all objects, that Beauty Absolute waits to be found and recognized by you, that you and all living beings are on a pilgrimage to discover Beauty Absolute or God.

VII

Sit comfortably and take any name of God that you love. OM is one of the highest and carries the most wonderful and universal vibrations of all —but take any name you like. Repeat it several times, and then imagine that a bright light is shining in your breast, in the heart-centre. Imagine that it is shining up into the throat. Now let it rise into the brain and issue from the head, spreading in all directions, carrying illumination with it. Send forth the rays with thoughts of friendliness and compassion to all. Do this for twenty minutes or upwards.

VIII

The following practice is a good one, and it helps to illumine the *chakras*, or occult centres of the body:

Sitting in your meditation posture, think of God. Now put the word OM in the throat-centre, and visualize it as a radiant light, part of which is shining upwards and the other part shining downwards, like a lamp on a threshold.

IX

Try to meditate on motion—not on moving objects, but on motion. In the *Platonic Dialogues*, attempts are made to express such abstract things. If you can extract the properties from their objects, and you meditate on those properties, then you are meditating, according to Plato, on Reality, which is ultimately the Archetype of the world of Forms. This is the Platonic world of Reality, which *Plotinus* adopted as the Kingdom of Heaven. Meditate on motion ; then, at a given moment, turn motion into light. Then meditate on light—not on a lighted object—but on light. Ultimately, meditate on the Self (*Atman*).

GENERAL REMARKS.

Devotion to God is one of the surest ways of purifying the will and intellect. At the time of devotion, you subject the mind to a stream of light—all your thoughts are centred on light. If your devotion is to Christ, then you are facing a great mountain of spiritual light, and it is the same with devotion to Rama, to Krishna, to Shri Dada. Devotion means projection of the best in you, in thought-form, to cover the holy figure of God or the Guru. In this psychological state, your mind is deluged with light, which has a cumulative effect, and even after meditation it lingers like the fragrance of a rose which you have once touched in a garden.

Do not struggle too much : create peace, suspend the mental machinery by devotion and meditation, and then the heart will be purified of itself. In the highest meditation there is no will, but there is a slow unification of the mind with some holy thought. When meditation is practised regularly and seriously the thought of the meditation possesses the mind, the will is allowed to sleep, desires become inactive, and passions are crushed with the hammer of " It is all illusion ". Thus is the will suspended. By this practice of suspension of the will in meditation, it is strengthened for everyday life. It is a great lesson to learn how to suspend the will when faced with the desire to do something which is spiritually wrong.

We must abandon everything that agitates or fatigues the mind, for in its natural state the mind is not fatigued. The muscular system has a bearing on the mind, and when it is fatigued the mind is fatigued also, and the converse is also true. One must not allow the mind to become fatigued, but real study, real devotion, never tire it. What tires the mind is to use it unnaturally, only for making money, for pleasure and so forth. The imprudent expenditure of sense-energy is one of the main causes of mental strain. Argument must not be irritable, and must only be resorted to in order to defend the truth, or to examine a statement to see whether it is true or not. Anger and infatuation must be avoided at all costs, and this can be done through meditation, or devotion to an Incarnation of God.

ADVANCED MEDITATION

Yoga is defined by *Patanjali* as the restraint of the mind, in order to create spiritual absorption. The restraint of the mind saves it from affliction, and produces the cognitive and ultracognitive spiritual absorption. The truth is known by the faculty which is dormant in an ordinary mind, but which is produced by restraining it, and which *Patanjali* calls *Ritambhara*, and others *Prajna*.

The ultimate means by which the mind is restrained are : *Continuous practice*, and *Non-attachment to what is passing*. These two methods are to be adopted as much as possible.

For those who have seriously begun to study meditation, and who have achieved some measure of purification and non-attachment, the following practices form the steps to higher meditation : *Austerity*, *Study* and *Self-surrender to God*.

AUSTERITY (*Tapas*)

This means the voluntary undergoing of sufferings and difficulties in order to strengthen the will and purify the heart. To habituate the body to the pairs of opposites, such as heat and cold, occasionally to sit up for several hours during the night, to perform spiritual exercises, to fast once a month, to speak the truth regardless of consequences—all this is austerity. A full description of austerity is given in the seventeenth chapter of the Gita.

Patanjali says : " The object of austerity is to destroy for ever the *sanskaras*, past impressions lying latent, arising from the network of sense-contacts with objects." These impressions have been accumulating in the causal body of man for incarnations, and they prevent the yogi from attaining liberation. The way to obliterate them is austerity, and there is no other way.

Vyasa, commenting on this verse of *Patanjali*, says : " Austerity must not be a destroyer of mental composure." This is an important point. The mind should rest in composure, and *tapas* must be done without destroying that composure. This requires great will-power. If the mental composure is broken, then the austerity is of a lower order, and the benefits obtained from it are dubious. Spiritual *tapas* arouses the sleeping powers of the will of man, and by applying the will on his own mind, he is able to educate and subdue it ; then the unknown powers of the mind awaken. Those who do not perform austerity do not acquire success in Yoga.

STUDY (*Svadhyaya*)

In the yogic sense, this means mastering spiritual classics, and also repetition of the word OM with concentrated attention. OM is the highest name of God ; to the one who does not believe in a personal God, it represents the ultimate Truth and Reality, which he desires to know. Repetition of this word, with meditation on its meaning, is essential for the yogi. Comprehension of the meaning through a study of the classics, sitting in a secluded place repeating the holy word rhythmically and slowly and concentrating the mind on it, are practices which, in some cases after a few months, cause the mind to pass into a high state of consciousness. OM is the highest mantra, and if the yogi is in the habit of repeating any other name of God in his devotion, he should add OM to it : by so doing, his mind will come to rest one-pointedly in God.

SELF-SURRENDER (*Ishvara-pranidhana*)

Self-surrender to God means dedication of all actions to Him, and offering the mind to Him. Like a stream of oil poured out without intermission from one vessel to another, the yogi pours his whole life into God or OM. He has ceaseless devotion to Him, in the form of OM if he cannot accept any other form.

There are three degrees of self-surrender to God. The first is the thought that He is all, the Spirit immanent in all. The second is the thought that He is in the mind. The meaning is that He is manifest in the mind, just as electricity is everywhere, but is particularly manifest in the bulb that gives the light. The third degree is the conviction : He is my Self, He and I are one. The first of these degrees is for meditation and benevolence, the second for meditation and mind-control, and the third is the end of meditation.

Of the three preliminaries, *Vyasa* gives the highest place to self-surrender. He says : " Self-surrender to God leads to austerity and study." Austerity and study by themselves do not necessarily lead to self-surrender, but if self-surrender is earnestly performed, then the tendencies to austerity and study appear of themselves. Furthermore, Patanjali says : " Self-surrender to God leads to spiritual absorption." Three times in his great classic on Yoga is this statement made—that complete surrender to God leads the yogi to his goal, even without other means.

The practice of austerity, study and self-surrender to God or to Truth, removes the erroneous cognitions which stand in the way of perfection. The erroneous cognitions are : ignorance (*avidya*), egoity, hatred, attachment, clinging to life. All these are offshoots of the first-named—ignorance—which is defined as " the erroneous cognition of everlastingness, purity, delight, and the self in what is temporal, impure, painful, and not the Self."

When the erroneous cognitions are active, they confirm the action of the three *gunas*, open the current of cause and effect (*Karma*), and produce action, birth, death and bondage. When they are no longer active, then by meditation the ultra-cognitive faculties are aroused, and the yogi beholds the true light which is the nature of the Self. Then the Self, the Spirit, is established in Its own nature, which is purity and bliss.

In this state of spiritual absorption no thing is cognized. All the cognizing faculties of the mind are withdrawn, restrained and evaporated within it. The mind is then comparable to a stage from which all the actors have made their exit. The actors are not there, the producer and promoter of the play are not there, the musicians of the orchestra are not there. Only the light shines, illuminating the empty stage. In this state of mind arises the ultra-cognitive faculty, and a bliss which is incomparable. All the riddles of existence are solved, and what remains is perfect bliss, perfect delight and perfect power. This is the goal of the holy Yoga.

POSTURE (*Asana*)

When the yogi has attained some degree of non-attachment to what is passing, and is earnestly engaged in austerity, study and self-surrender to God, he begins the practice of true meditation. Seated in a place free from distraction and interruptions, in a comfortable posture which he can maintain for a long time without moving, with head, neck and spine in a straight line, he practises relaxation. This is done by breathing deeply and slowly, mentally repeating OM, one half during the in-breath, and the second half during the out-breath. With each out-breath he relaxes his muscles and nerves. By relaxation, steadiness of posture is achieved.

WITHDRAWAL (*Pratyahara*)

The senses are now to be withdrawn from all outer stimuli, and the mind from all passing thoughts which are useless for spiritual progress. This does not mean total withdrawal in the sense of inertia. The mind is engaged in spiritual practices, in the things which have a spiritual value, and there can be no withdrawal from the service of the spiritual Teacher, and Truth, from study and from the spiritual group to which the yogi belongs.

CONCENTRATION (*Dharana*)

The Sanskrit word for concentration is *Dharana*, from a root meaning to maintain or support. It means the restricting of the mind-stream to one point. Concentration is generally first made on an object gross or subtle. Later on the yogi may meditate on thought itself and on the Self. The further stages, *Dhyana* and *Samadhi*, now to be described, follow in each case. The process is first set out as it applies to concentration on a gross object. Note that the form of an Incarnation is included under the heading of " gross object " because it consists of " name and form ".

To practise concentration, the yogi chooses an object, for instance a flower, and focusses his attention on it. Its size, colour, form, weight, and all other attributes are to be reduced to a point, and kept before him as an idea. Any particular thought of its colour or form and so on, will involve a succession of ideas, which the yogi wishes to avoid. The yogic tradition is that the best focus for the mind is the form of the spiritual Teacher as an idea of the Lord, as the centre of the cosmic ideation. If he has not yet found a Teacher, he concentrates on the form of one of the Incarnations of the Lord, such as Christ or Krishna, or if he cannot do that, then on the word OM. This word, representing Truth, can be visualized as written on the heart of the yogi. Higher levels of consciousness are reached by these practices.

DHYANA

Dhyana, or meditation, is a step beyond concentration. When concentration has been practised for some time, there is continuous flow of the mind-stream unbroken by any other cognition, upon the object, and this is *dhyana*. The nature of the object of concentration is gross : when *dhyana* reaches maturity, gross matter disappears and leaves in its place the subtle infra-atomic constituents which make up the ultimate elements of matter. The ability to perceive this subtle background of matter depends on the purity of the concentrating mind and, for this reason, the preliminary practices are essential before meditation is undertaken. In *dhyana*, consciousness of the outer world is lost, but it still may be restored by a strong stimulus from without. The next stage, *Samadhi*, is not broken by any outer event. After *dhyana*, the yogi who is devoted to his Teacher attains *Samadhi* or identificative contemplation.

SAMADHI

When, under the influence of the object meditated upon, the meditation becomes free from all separate notions of meditation, object of meditation and meditator, and continues to subsist entirely in the form of the object of meditation, the state is called Conscious *Samadhi*.[1] Relative or total loss of subject-object consciousness produces the Conscious *Samadhi*. It is of four kinds :—

In the lowest kind of Conscious *Samadhi*, the mind is one with the object, but also with the concept of the object, and with its name. This fusion of object, concept and name is technically known as " deliberation ", and the lowest grade of *Samadhi* is called " *Samadhi* with deliberation ".

Higher than this first grade is the *Samadhi* in

[1] *Samadhi* may roughly be translated as identificative contemplation, or communion, but the Sanskrit term is precise and more convenient.

which the association of name and concept is discarded. Here there is a vague union of the subject and object, but now the object is just object without predicative relationship. The highest part of the mind, *buddhi*, still functions, because the subtle constituents of the object still remain, but the grossness of the object is no longer felt.

In the next grade, the subtle constituents of matter vanish, and also time. This *Samadhi* has as its associate joy and is called the Joyous or Blissful *Samadhi*.

In the highest grade of Conscious *Samadhi*, the yogi finally attains in the same object, the direct perception of Self, of the form of pure Consciousness. The spiritual Teacher tells the pupil at the right time, when he should see the supreme Self in place of the object of meditation. By means of the meditation, and by the grace of the Teacher, the yogi realizes that he is the Self, the canvas on which the picture of the world is painted by illusion.

MEDITATION ON THE PROCESS OF THOUGHT

Meditation is also performed, if the Teacher directs, on the process of thought, and on the Knower, which is the Spirit or Self. The Teacher gives the pupil texts and practices, which embody the type of meditation suitable to his stage of advancement.

In the meditation on the process of thought, the mind is turned on itself, becoming a disinterested witness of its own activity. See yourself for a while ; be fixed in the principle : " I am the Spirit, free from change and qualities, ever blissful." Let the thoughts take their own course; the mind may behave like an irrational monkey, but just witness it—do not worry—think that you are watching a comedian performing on a stage. Day by day the irrational activities will become less. You may have thousands of thoughts during the first twelve weeks, but the number progressively decreases. Then observe introspectively how certain thoughts appear; observe the rise, development and disappearance of the selected ideas.

The next development is the careful observation of the interval between successive thoughts. The aim of the practice is to make the mind-stream calm and still. Thoughts of all kinds are to be eliminated. The practice is recommended in the classic called " Yoga Vasishtha ". Unless the preliminary practices have been faithfully done, the latent desires and impressions will bristle up at this stage to disturb the mind-stream, like seeds sown in spring coming up in the autumn. By earnest and intense practice and the grace of the Teacher, these disturbances are removed, and all desire and aversion vanishes. Then, in the Samadhi which is the interval between thoughts, the Self is seen. The pure Self is comparable to the thread of a necklace on which every bead is a thought. The thread runs through all the beads but, being covered by them, its existence is not evident. When the gap between two thoughts is observed and prolonged, the blissful Self is comprehended in the process of knowledge, just as when Samadhi was made on an object, the Self was realised in the object.

The object of all study and introspective effort

in *Yoga*, is to make the mind thought-free. The real life begins when thoughts are consciously suppressed. Repetition of the word OM innumerable times is a practice whereby the mental vacuum may be produced.

MEDITATION ON SELF

In the direct meditation on the Knower or Self, the Yogi meditates on the great sentences which teach non-duality, such as " That Thou Art " (*Tat Twam Asi*), and "I am Brahman" (*Aham Brahmasmi*). This is the highest form of meditation. *Shri Shankara* speaks of it in the verse : " The wise man should attentively meditate on his own Self, which though unseen, is yet the only reality ; and manifest in the external universe, is yet of the nature of subjective consciousness." And again : " *Samadhi* whose other name is Knowledge, is the forgetfulness of all mental activity, by first making thought changeless and then identifying the consciousness with Brahman."

SUPRA-CONSCIOUS SAMADHI

The goal of the meditation practice is to immobilize the attention spontaneously, and the role of the will is to be carefully noted. Mental relaxation induced by meditation, and especially by the proximity of the spiritual Teacher, with full faith in him, leads to the elimination of effort and progressive disappearance of the individual will. In the last stage of Conscious *Samadhi*, there is complete vacuity of mind, and disappearance of the will, acquired consciously.

The ultimate goal of the yogi—spiritual absorption

—means complete transcendence of the mind-stuff. The state in which there is a total severance of Consciousness (Self) from the mind, is called Supra-conscious *Samadhi*. *Prakriti* (matter), though illusory, binds as it were the Self, which is Reality, through the mind-stuff. But when the mind-stuff is transcended, the sense of individual personality goes and then the Self abides in His own nature. The Gita says : " They who by the eye of wisdom perceive the distinction between matter and Self, and the dissolution of matter, which is the cause of beings—they reach the Supreme." *Shri Shankara*, in his commentary on this verse, says : " They who in this manner perceive the exact distinction between matter and Self, by the eye of wisdom which has been generated by the teachings of the Scriptures and of the spiritual Teacher, and who also perceive the non-existence of *Prakriti*, the material cause of beings—they reach *Brahman*, the Real, the supreme Self, and assume no more bodies."

The state of Supra-conscious *Samadhi* does not last all the time, but its memory abides, like the fragrance of roses which lingers even after they have been discarded. On this, *Swami Rama Tirtha*, one of the greatest yogis of modern India, says : "All creeds are simply efforts to rend asunder the veil which covers our eyes. Some have succeeded in making the veil thinner than others, but in all religions there are people who have the Truth, and whenever the true spirit comes, then, whether the curtain be thick or thin, it is pushed aside for the time being, and a glimpse into Reality is obtained. The curtain is drawn aside, but it falls before the eyes again. If it is thick, it again veils Reality, but if it has been rendered extremely thin, then, even though it be not thrust aside, it does not prevent our seeing Reality. We can see through it, and we can also remove it altogether at times. *Vedanta* reduces the curtain of ignorance to its thinnest, and enables the illumined man to enjoy the blissful vision even in everyday life. The votaries of all religions can at times lift the veil, whether thick or thin, from before their eyes. The *Vedantin* also can do that, but he enjoys the vision of Reality even in the ordinary state, which those who follow creeds of thicker veil do not." Those saints who think of their self and God in terms of " I am His ", keep the curtain in its thickest form. The curtain is thinner in religions of the form of " I am Thine ". The thinnest curtain is in the form " I am He ". Even if the curtain be before the eyes, in this form it is so thin that Reality can be seen through it.

In order to fulfil the holy tradition, yogis descend through their mind to become teachers, serving their own Self in others. They take up their bodies for the natural term of life, thus raising the curtain again before their eyes. But it is so thin that, even while living in the world, they enjoy uninterrupted union with the Supreme. They see the whole world as a conjurer's show, as a conscious dream, and enjoy unbroken bliss. The Lord says in the Gita, " The illumined man is my very Self."

CONCLUSION

The great commentators on the yoga texts say that the meditations should proceed step by step from the simpler practices to the profound. There is, however, an important qualification. In special cases it is found that, through the grace of God, or through the favour of the spiritual Teacher, the aspirant to liberation is from the outset capable of practising the more subtle stages, and, in such cases, he need not waste time in traversing the preliminary steps, because the attainment of the lower stages, which is the sole end of the earlier practices, has already been accomplished.

" The sequence ", say *Vijnana Bhikshu*, " as given, is the normal one, the reason being that the mind cannot all at once enter into that which is the highest, most subtle essence." The commentators and the great saints and sages of both ancient and modern times all agree that advanced meditation is to be practised under the direction of a traditional Teacher who sees the heart of the disciple and is able to give the help which is needed at the critical stages of the process.

*   *   *

In the *Chandogya Upanishad*, the Teacher says to his pupil : " My son, go and bring me a *Nyagrodha* [banyan] fruit." The pupil goes, because obedience is one of the highest virtues in a spiritual sense. He brings the fruit and the Teacher says : " Open it." He opens it and finds tiny seeds within it, hundreds and thousands of them. The Teacher then says : " My son, what is each seed here ? Is not each seed a tree?—each containing millions of fruits, and in each fruit, further millions ; is it not so ? "

The disciple replies : " It is so." The Teacher

says to the boy: "Now meditate thus, my son:

"I meditate on Him Whose body is the earth, on Him Whose sight is fire, Whose mind is light, Who is the resort of all human souls. I meditate on Him."

This is a text from the *Shruti*, and the Teacher and disciple then meditate together on this text. Apollo is driving his chariot with seven horses furiously on the horizon; clouds appear, gather and disperse; the wind blows hard, but still the Teacher and pupil continue their meditation together. Now the pupil is meditating on the Teacher, and then on the essence in the Teacher, which is one with the universal Essence. After a while, he rises and says: " Yes, my Lord, I have seen that the divine Essence is within me."

This is the way of meditation given in the *Upanishads* and the *Gita*. Those who have thus received the time-honoured and eternal meditations, they have a million more advantages than those to whom the Truth has been taught in words—a million more.

A father loved one of his sons more than the others. He gave horses and bullocks, gold and silver, and large tracts of his property to the other sons, but to the favoured one he gave only an eighth of an acre of land. " This is for you, my son," he said. The son was a disciple and therefore answered: " So be it, my father." Then the father said to him: " Plough it and dig it very carefully." After digging it for a long time, the son found a chest full of most precious diamonds. Such are the meditations granted by the spiritual Teacher to his pupils—they will yield fruit some day.

Key Books on Yoga

by Hari Prasad Shastri

THE HEART OF THE EASTERN
MYSTICAL TEACHING

WISDOM FROM THE EAST

SEARCH FOR A GURU

YOGA (*Foyles Handbook*)

THE CREST JEWEL OF WISDOM
translated by A J Alston
with Dr Shastri's commentary

by Marjorie Waterhouse

TRAINING THE MIND
THROUGH YOGA

THE POWER BEHIND THE MIND

WHAT YOGA HAS TO OFFER

Recently published

A SHORT COURSE OF MEDITATION